Good Afternoon Vietnam

A CIVILIAN IN THE VIETNAM WAR

Gary L. Wilhelm

COPYRIGHT © 2017 BY GARY L. WILHELM

All rights reserved. No part of this publication may be reproduced, distributed or transmitted in any form or by any means, including photocopying, recording, or other electronic or mechanical methods, without the prior written permission of the publisher, except in the case of brief quotations embodied in critical reviews and certain other noncommercial uses permitted by copyright law. For permission requests, write to the publisher, addressed "Attention: Permissions Coordinator," at https://frugal-engineer.com/contact/

Gary L Wilhelm

Maple Grove, MN 55369

http://frugal-engineer.com

Book Layout ©2017 BookDesignTemplates.com

Ordering Information:

Quantity sales. Special discounts are available on quantity purchases by corporations, associations, and others. For details, contact the "Special Sales Department" at https://frugalengineer.com/contact/

Good Afternoon Vietnam: A Civilian in the Vietnam War/ Gary L. Wilhelm. —1st ed.

Photos by Gary L. Wilhelm

Cover Design by http://www.surferkiddies.com/

US Government Online Copyright Registration Number TXu002069991

ISBN-10: 0692999906
ISBN-13: 978-0692999905

Find the free discussion guide for secondary education at this link: https://www.thewiseowlfactory.com/good-afternoon-vietnam-book-review-and-free-guide/

Dedication
To Theo: May Your Life Be Free of War

ACKNOWLEDGEMENTS

Thank you to my writing group for listening to some of these stories and making suggestions. Thank you to family and friends who patiently read and reread the stories, making comments and suggestions. Special thanks to Carolyn, whose encouragement and internet expertise made this possible.

Contents

INTRODUCTION: GOOD AFTERNOON VIETNAM. 1
HAPPENSTANCE..11
DaNANG VIA NORTH CAROLINA 13
CLEANING LAUNDRY LADY...................................17
COMMUNICATIONS AND TRAVEL 19
SAFETY..23
GEORGE'S SAD ODYSSEY......................................25
MY VERY OWN TRANSPORTATION?.....................29
HOLIDAY SEASON – 1968--DaNANG 33
AIR CONDITIONING..39
SUBSTITUTE TEACHER 43
HOA KHANH CHILDREN'S HOSPITAL.....................45
DaNANG BOMB DUMP EXPLODES........................49
WHEN PIGS FLY 55
SOUTHEAST ASIA PHOTO JOURNAL 59
MARINE CORPS BIRTHDAY PARTY 1969 79
SURPRISE OFFER FROM THE CLEANING LAUNDRY LADY..81
GOING HOME 83
CONCLUSIONS 85
ABOUT THE AUTHOR 91
REVIEWS 93

CHAPTER 1

INTRODUCTION: GOOD AFTERNOON VIETNAM

It was a clear sunny day in May 1968, and I was on a large commercial airplane chartered from Continental Airlines by the U.S government. I could look out the window and see a coral reef below in the ocean near the coast of South Vietnam. I had never before been outside the U.S much less seen a coral reef. I took a picture of it from the airplane window; it would be many months before I took another picture. All the other seats on the airplane were filled with military people in uniform.

Gary L. Wilhelm

I was a young civilian engineer working for Univac, the St. Paul based computer company. The plan was for Univac to have two engineers on site with the system; the second engineer was to come in two weeks. No one else from my part of Univac had previously gone to Vietnam and been available to tell me what to expect. Although it wasn't my first choice, I had agreed to go there because I had heard so much about it ... pro and con ... and I was curious to see it for myself. In preparation, the company had me take many shots ... for cholera, plague, yellow fever, typhoid, and others. I had spent many months training with the newly developed electronic intelligence (Elint) system, using a Univac computer to analyze Elint data in minutes rather than days or weeks, as with previous, manual systems. Elint data was collected by our reconnaissance planes flying near enemy weapon systems. They would come back from their mission with information on tapes that required analysis. After analysis we would know which enemy weapon systems were out there and exactly where they were located. The extent of my preparation was this system familiarization and the long list of immunizations. I was dressed as if I were going to my engineering job back in the U.S. wearing a blue suit, white shirt, and tie.

So now I was on my way to MAG 11 (Marine Air Group 11) located in DaNang, South Vietnam. The Elint system in two vans each the size of a one car garage was on its way too ... in a separate cargo plane. Two large vans were needed because computer equipment was much larger then, than it is today. This had been a long journey: a 45 minute refueling stop in Hawaii, another stop in Okinawa for hours while the airplane was repaired and test flown, but now we were almost there.

We came in at high altitude, dived toward the DaNang airport, and made what seemed like a high speed landing. As we went down the runway, I looked out the window and saw warplanes in revetments (earth or concrete to separate one airplane from another in case one was hit by an incoming rocket and exploded) flash by; many were camouflaged, and my impression was that the whole place looked very ominous.

We taxied up to a ramshackled wooden building with some wooden fenced areas out in front. In one of these fenced-in areas were troops anxiously waiting to get on our plane to go home. The pilot turned off the engines; steps were rolled up to the plane, and the flight attendants opened the doors ... good afternoon Vietnam. We were instructed to deplane quickly. As I approached the door, I thought I was standing in front of a hot oven. It was early afternoon in May, and the heat and humidity were unbearable ... the place didn't smell very good either. I really could not believe life could exist in conditions like this. I think I was almost in a state of shock ... this was going to be really bad. My picture of the coral reef was the last picture I would take for months because I really didn't think I would ever want to remember anything I was seeing.

When the passengers were all on the tarmac, an army sergeant greeted us: "OK, Army over here, Air Force over there, and Marines in this area." There I stood in my blue suit, white shirt, and tie. I decided I better go with the Marines to find MAG 11. We climbed into the back of a "six-by" open truck, which took us away. Although a few civilian airplanes did come into DaNang airport, it was basically a huge military base and one of the busiest airports in the world at that time. On one side of the runways were the Marines, a Navy recon group, the bomb storage area, and a refugee village, which was referred to as Dogpatch even in U.S. newspapers. On the other side was the Air Force, a CIA transportation/supply group known as Air

America, and South Vietnamese military units and officials.

Eventually the truck arrived at the MAG 11 living area. It was totally fenced in and enclosed with razor concertina wire. Just inside the gate was a sign with a number indicating the current condition: 4 was no activity, 3 was on alert, 2 was attack imminent, and 1 for under attack. When I arrived the number was 4. Once inside the gate, I went to the MAG 11 headquarters building to check in. I was immediately given a steel helmet, a bullet proof (flack) jacket, and a gas mask to go with my blue suit, white shirt, and necktie.

I was then assigned a bunk in a small screened-in hut in the officer quarters area. There were four people in each hut. No running water, but there was a communal water faucet outside for every few huts. The huts had limited electricity. There was an open-air urinal, and a screened in toilet area.

There was also one communal shower for all the officers.

The enlisted men lived in an adjacent living area in the same size screened in huts; however, there were more enlisted people in each hut ... I think 12 instead of 4. There were a few enclosed huts with air conditioning, but only for pilots, who often had to fly at night. I was given mosquito netting to set up over my bunk at night, to avoid getting malaria. The alternative was to have a window fan attached to the foot of your bunk to blow on you all night in order to keep the mosquitoes away. I had not brought a window fan with me, so I had to use the netting for awhile.

Another essential was a small box with a light bulb inside. It was necessary to put shoes and clothes inside this box at night. This prevented mold and mildew from growing on your shoes and clothes during the night. If this box was not used, green fuzz would grow during a single night. There were cockroaches ... big ones. One of my new roommates joked "If you throw your boot at the cockroaches, they throw it back at you."

Later in the afternoon, I was given military fatigues to wear in order to blend in with the Marines; because enemy snipers occasionally infiltrated Dogpatch and fired into our area. I had an equivalent military rank of major and civilian insignia to wear, but no weapon. I was instructed to take one malaria pill per week and salt tablets every day.

When darkness came, the sky came alive with planes circling the base and dropping flares suspended from parachutes to light up areas on the periphery of the base. There were C 130 gunships circling also, and periodically they would turn their GAU Gatling guns on in order to fire at potential enemy near the base. These guns were very noisy ... reminding me of the sound of a high-powered racing car engine during a race. There would be a solid red line from the plane to the target on the ground caused by the tracer bullets from the gun. These sights and sounds were surreal, but by this time I was exhausted, went to sleep, and slept through the night. The next day I thought I heard thunder, but the sky was clear. One of the Marines informed me, "no that was a B52 bombing strike nearby ... code named an Arclight."

It was not until the middle of my third night in DaNang that I experienced my first enemy attack. The sirens went off, someone was yelling "INCOMING" over a loudspeaker system, and then loud "crack, crack, crack" sounds as the rockets came in, and exploded spraying white-hot pieces of shrapnel through the air ... and through anything they hit. What had I gotten myself into? It was already clear to me that no matter how much I had seen on TV, movies, or read; until I was actually present to begin to see, hear, smell, and feel war, I really did not have any understanding of it.

I did not know then that I would not make it back to the USA until late 1969.

CHAPTER 2

HAPPENSTANCE

After my arrival, I had time to think about the sequence of events that led up to my ending up in DaNang. The first company I worked for after college unexpectedly lost their largest account which amounted to more than 60% of their business. A large reduction in force was necessary for them to survive. I along with many other people was laid off. Fortunately the job market for engineers was good at that time, but I really did want to find another position as quickly as possible.

I got several job offers quickly, and ended up accepting an offer from a large company named Univac, which had informed me they were hiring for a government contract they were expecting next week. At that time it was common practice to hire in anticipation of contracts. I and two other engineers accepted offers for the anticipated contract. I arrived earlier in the morning than the other two, and was assigned my own desk. When they arrived there was only one other desk left, so they had to share it. Weeks went by, and the contract still had not arrived. The other two sharing the desk soon left, and I became bored and started looking for another job within the company where I could be productive. I learned Univac urgently needed an engineer for an existing job located in Reykjavik, Iceland. I thought this would be interesting, as I had not been out of the U.S. before. I went to my supervisor and asked to transfer and take the job. The response was: "No, the contract is coming and we will need you here," Months went by and still no contract. I had a desk and was being paid, but no work to do. Eventually I was told "Ok you can transfer," I went back and asked for that job in Iceland. I was told: "Sorry we had to fill that job with someone else, but we have this other need now ... which will mean going to Vietnam after some system testing at the Cherry Point Marine Corps Air Station in North Carolina," So I started out agreeing to go to Iceland, and through "Happenstance" I was on my way to Vietnam instead.

CHAPTER 3

DaNANG VIA NORTH CAROLINA

Univac shipped two of our systems to the Marine Corps Air Station at Cherry Point, N.C. for six months of further testing in N.C., before one of the systems would be shipped to Marine Air Group 11 in DaNang, South Vietnam. Three Univac engineers were sent to N.C. to participate in this testing. We stayed at a motel on an outer bank about 20 miles from the Marine base. From our motel on the outer bank, we had a really good view of several hurricanes while we were there. We also had an experience when driving on a four lane highway, back from work at the base to our motel one Friday night. I was sitting in the back seat and the other two Univac people were in the front seat, when flashing blue lights came on behind us. We were being stopped by the N.C. highway patrol. The state patrol officer told the driver he had been exceeding the speed limit by

5 miles per hour. Since the car had Minnesota license plates and the driver had a Minnesota driver's license, he would have to take the driver to jail in the next town. He put the driver in the back of his patrol car, and drove off.

I moved to the driver's spot in our car and followed the patrol car. We arrived at the jail and went inside; the scene was right out of a B rated black and white movie about the South. It was a small really dirty place with two fat deputies sitting beside a small stove for heat. There was an old dog laying nearby, too. One of the deputies volunteered that since the bondsman was out of town for the weekend, our driver would be required to stay in jail until he returned. I asked: "Well, how much is the bail?" Forty dollars was the reply. I reached into my wallet and took out two $20 bills. Only then were we allowed to go on our way.

Testing and checkout of the systems also proved to be a challenge. Some of the subsystems purchased from other companies but incorporated into Univac's systems were not very reliable, and one of the two Univac systems was quite intermittent, and the Marines were becoming impatient, and rightly so.

Finally after a few months, I generated a multi-page report enumerating the problems and describing the issues in detail. I sent the report back to Univac in St. Paul, and it resulted in rather quick and decisive action. The main computer in the system which was intermittent had been produced during a strike by replacement workers that apparently were not well trained. Univac put pressure on the subsystem vendors, who needed to upgrade their units, and also flew an additional eight Univac personnel to North Carolina to deal with the intermittent computer. That team worked long hours going through the entire computer which had been built using taper pins. They pulled on every wire in the computer, and whenever a pin came loose, it was properly reseated. This process took days, but resulted in curing the system intermittence. At the end of this, Univac's Vice President came to NC for a big meeting where it was agreed we were ready to send one system to DaNang. All that was left was for me to get my Status of Forces card, which indicated I was civilian but had been granted the status of US forces in Vietnam. Then I was on my way to DaNang ... pretty much by happenstance.

What follows are my memories of occurrences during my time working in South Vietnam many years ago.

CHAPTER 4

CLEANING LAUNDRY LADY

The Marines hired Vietnamese ladies to come on the base during the day to sweep the sand out of our huts, and to wash our clothes by hand in metal cans, which had held ammunition and been discarded.

The first time my clothes were washed, everything came back clean except my black socks, which seemed to have disappeared. This was somewhat important because I could not just go to the sock store and buy new socks ... especially the good ones I liked to wear. So the next day I confronted the lady and told her I needed my socks back. She was very old and somewhat cantankerous, and didn't say much, but the next day my socks reappeared. After that we got along fine and she was the cleaning/laundry lady for my hut as long as I was there.

CHAPTER 5

COMMUNICATIONS AND TRAVEL

I soon learned that communication was somewhat limited. There was of course mail, but that required days. There was an amateur radio station, but that was for military personnel to be able to talk with their loved ones for a few minutes. However one could not pick up the phone and call the USA from Vietnam because this was a war zone. If it became necessary to have a telephone discussion with your company or anyone else, it required travel to another country outside the war zone, where a call was permitted. During my time there I made trips to Okinawa, Taiwan, Bangkok, and Singapore in order to communicate.

Usually this was a matter of almost hitch hiking on a flight that was leaving for another country, and often having to take a different flight back to

DaNang. On one occasion I took a C130 flight from Okinawa that was going back to DaNang. There was a really large wooden box on board. On the way back we landed on a very basic landing strip at DongHa, which is almost right on the border with North Vietnam. As soon as the plane came to a stop we were told to get out and get in the slit trenches by the side of the landing strip, while the large box was off loaded. We learned it was full of ammunition to resupply DongHa. Afterward we re-boarded the plane and took off for DaNang.

The street scene with automobiles is from Okinawa, which is in contrast with the swarms of mopeds, motorcycles, and even pedicabs in the streets of Vietnam. Also on Okinawa there were still Japanese concrete bunkers remaining from WWII. Although rather basic, these bunkers were really built to withstand war.

Another time I took an Air Vietnam old DC3 flight where one of the other passengers, an older Vietnamese woman came on board with a live chicken in a cardboard box ... no problem. It was always good to spend a few days in another country outside of the war zone. Coming back, it always took a few days to adjust again.

CHAPTER 6

SAFETY

Other than putting on a helmet and flak jacket and getting in a bunker during attacks, there was not much else to protect one from shrapnel or bullets. However there were other precautions I chose to take, such as not wandering around out in the village alone, and using very limited alcohol. There were guns everywhere, and I was glad for the armed Marines to protect me. The Vietnamese military also had weapons, and often manned checkpoints. Basically there were a lot of guns everywhere, and I didn't have one, and sometimes this felt uncomfortable.

I was not allowed to carry a weapon, but I did go with the Marine officers to the shooting range on Sunday afternoons in order to shoot and familiarize myself with military weapons (both ours and theirs).

This was in case of an emergency where I could pick up a weapon to defend myself. I wanted to be able to effectively use any weapon if it became necessary.

CHAPTER 7

GEORGE'S SAD ODYSSEY

About a month after I landed in DaNang, a new company representative arrived and was assigned to a bed in our hut. He was a representative from General Electric. His name was George and he was older than most of us there...in his 40's I think. He was a pleasant fellow and his job was to help the Marines with problems they were having with the diesel generators used to supply our electrical power. He informed us that he knew of another representative nearby, but located at a small, remote fire base.

Soon George received word that the other person at the remote fire base was quite ill, with dysentery. George was asked to stand by in case his assistance was needed. There was no further word for several weeks. Then George received word that his counterpart was being medevac'd to another area with better medical facilities, for treatment. Another week passed, and George received a letter from his company informing him that the other person had died. At the remote firebase, the person had become so dehydrated that he lapsed into a coma. The paper-work filled out at the firebase to have him medevac'd for better medical treatment, somehow sent him to the wrong location, which also had very limited medical facilities, rather than to a larger base with medical doctors. He was comatose and could not speak up for himself, to try to be redirected to reach a better medical facility in time.

George boarded a plane with the body to escort it back to the U.S. He was gone for two weeks. When he returned he had a large gash on his forehead with stitches still in place. When the plane landed bringing him back to DaNang, there was no ground transportation available to get him back to MAG 11. So he decided to try walking. A Chinese business man offered him a ride in an old jeep. Unfortunately they collided with a military truck, and George received a large gash that required stitches. George's sad odyssey was over.

CHAPTER 8

MY VERY OWN TRANSPORTATION?

Getting around in Vietnam was not easy. There was a shuttle running from the living area to the flight line and back every 15 minutes, where we could sit on a wooden bench in the back of a 6 by truck for the ride of about one mile. There was a tarp over the top so we could keep dry if it was raining. Other than that, it was "catch-as-catch-can" for getting around. The Marine PX (store) was about a mile away, and the Air Force PX was several miles, and it was sometimes necessary to buy tooth paste, soap, and other necessities. The Air Force PX was stocked much better. After George's experience being injured in an auto wreck while hitch hiking, I decided to try to obtain a small motorbike for getting around. I had heard stores in Japan would partially disassemble a motorbike and send it to DaNang via mail. One of my friends was going to Japan on a short trip. I gave him cash and asked him to have a shop there send me a motorbike. My motorbike arrived, was assembled, and I was mobile ... ah what freedom. I would ride to either PX whenever I wanted. Going to the Air Force PX I rode by a large supply depot. One of the notable things at this depot was a large quantity of aluminum caskets stacked up outside. I wondered how many of these would be used for people killed in battle? How many would be used for people, like the company rep who died of untreated disease, people killed in accidents, or for people who died in other ways? This pile of caskets reinforced what I already knew: that this was a dangerous place.

On one of my trips to the Air Force PX, I parked and locked my bike, went inside and made my purchases. When I came out, I noticed several ARVN (Vietnamese army guys) next to my bike. One of the ARVN was bent over trying to hot-wire my bike. They were unarmed, so I ran toward them. The one who was trying to hot-wire my bike hopped on the back of another bike and sped-off before I got there. A few minutes later, and I'm sure they would have been gone with my bike. Another ARVN, who had been standing nearby came over and said something like "that was a bad guy," I suspect he was in on it too. He asked me for a cigarette ... of course I had none. But I still had my bike and was able to get safely back to the Marine compound. This caused me to really think about whether it was a good idea to go alone by motorbike ... even to a PX a few miles away. Very often the ARVN were armed ... then what? Not to mention the other "bad guys" who might be around. I sold my motor bike and decided to not travel by motorbike even to PX's a few miles away.

CHAPTER 9

HOLIDAY SEASON - 1968--DaNANG

The holiday season in DaNang was a difficult time for several reasons ... some obvious and others not so obvious. For one thing, the weather was basically a monsoon season. The sky was usually gray and there was rain on most days ... a lot of rain. I seem to recall that in the month of November there had been 60 inches of rainfall. There was water everywhere. One had to be careful when walking to avoid deep holes filled with water. In the officer's club people would break out singing "we got to get out of this place if it's the last thing we ever do" or the other "anthem" "green, green grass of home" more frequently than usual.

Down at the flight line, silver napalm containers were stacked up to form a small wall, and written on that wall in bold red paint were the words

"Merry Xmas HoHoHo," Of course the leader of North Vietnam was Ho Chi Minh. Napalm containers were filled with flammable liquid. They were loaded on our planes and basically used to firebomb enemy positions.

We did have tapes of Christmas music, which we played inside our ELINT van. And the effect of that music in that time and place was quite amazing. It was a little taste of home, and it really brought tears to one's eyes ... happy tears. I think the feeling is indescribable unless one has "been there and done that."

On New Year's Eve, I was sound asleep in my hut when I was suddenly awakened by the other engineer from Univac. John was crying ... with tears streaming down his face. He was extremely upset, and also clearly alcohol impaired. Finally he told me that he had been drinking and playing cards with others in a hut several hundred feet away. One of the Marines there pulled his pistol, put it against the back of John's head, marched him outside and said he was going to kill him.

Obviously the Marine did not follow through with his threat, but this is what happened to John causing him to come to my hut and wake me up. I listened to John for awhile and tried to calm him down. I said I didn't see anyone coming to kill him now, suggested he go back to his hut and try to get some sleep, and we would talk more about it in the morning. John had previous alcohol problems in DaNang which I will say more about later. I was tired and went back to sleep.

In the morning John was nowhere to be found. I learned that he had "hopped" an early morning C130 flight to Okinawa that was due to return the next day. John did come back the next day, and explained that he had called our supervisor, Henry in St. Paul. After he described the incident, Henry persuaded John to come back to DaNang, and tell me to call the company to discuss what to do. Of course we could not make phone calls from Vietnam because it was an active war zone and there were security issues. It was necessary to fly out of the war zone and call from another country. I learned there was a flight going to Bangkok in two days and I was able to get a seat on that flight. I flew to Bangkok and called Henry right away. Henry wanted to know if I thought John was really in danger. I told him I didn't think so, but I was not present at the incident and didn't know for sure. Henry said they had made a decision to pull John out of DaNang, but that it would take some time to do so.

In the meantime, I had a few days in Bangkok before my scheduled return flight to DaNang. I did some sightseeing in the city and on the canals of Bangkok. There were many beautiful Buddhist temples and other interesting sights to see. It was a very nice break from Vietnam ... a whole different environment. There was a small band providing musical entertainment in one of the restaurants. All of the instruments were made from bamboo. As I was eating, some uniformed U.S. servicemen came in the door. The band launched into a medley of Air Force, Army, Navy, and Marine songs ... with their bamboo instruments. I ended up buying a couple of the instruments to take home with me. One was a reed instrument made with a little pitch to hold the bamboo together. The other was a percussion instrument.

When I returned to DaNang, I learned John was gone. He had been medevac'd out of Vietnam. He was involved in an accident (nothing to do with combat or violence) and badly broke his arm. I never did learn exactly what led up to the New Year's Eve incident, but it was evident that a lot of alcohol was involved. I did learn who had pulled the gun on John. It was a Marine, who was frequently at the officer's club sitting and drinking alone at the end of the bar. Several months previously, I had sat down beside him, ordered a drink and had a brief conversation with him. He told me he was married to a Japanese woman and they had two children. His wife and children were in Japan. I asked him: "Japan? Not the U.S.?" He said he thought they were better off in Japan ... which surprised me. That's all I knew about him. After the incident, I do not recall seeing him again. I don't know whether he was transferred, went to the brig, or what. About a week after I returned to DaNang, the executive officer of the group joined me in the mess hall at lunch to briefly discuss the incident. I think he mainly wanted to know if the company planned to take any action. They did not. I always felt safe because of the Marines, and was glad they were armed, except in the officer's club. At the officer's club weapons had to be left in the coat room. I was a noncombatant and not allowed to carry a weapon; however I went with the Marines to the shooting range on several Sunday afternoons, in order to familiarize myself with, and practice with military weapons ... assault rifles, grenade launchers, heavy machine guns, and even weapons the enemy used. I was surprised at how "tinny" the enemy AK47's sounded, but I knew the AK47 was very reliable and effective. I felt that if it ever became necessary for me to use a weapon, I could pick one up, and I would know how to use it.

Earlier I mentioned John's other problems at DaNang. One night, he had drunkenly staggered across the compound, becoming entangled in the concertina razor wire protecting the commanding officer's house and command station. This sounded an alarm and the Marine guards came out with their weapons pointed at him. When they saw who it was, they began laughing. He became angry and threatened to sue the Marine corp. The guards picked him up and took him to the dispensary to have his cuts treated. Another time, John had been drinking with some enlisted men. He persuaded a Marine, who was not an officer, to go with him to the officer's club. That did not go over well either. Even realizing how difficult holidays are in a war zone and knowing some of John's previous history, I was really unprepared for the New Year's Eve incident!

CHAPTER 10

AIR CONDITIONING

In early 1969, former military man, Jim Y, the other newly arrived Univac engineer Dean O, another civilian from MacDonald Douglas, and I decided to move into a screened-in hut that had been vacated. Rockets with explosive warheads were attached to our planes and could be fired from the air at enemy positions on the ground. These rockets were packed with Styrofoam to protect them during shipment. Our plan was to use discarded Styrofoam from rocket packaging to enclose and insulate this hut. Our dream was then maybe we could get an air conditioner and make the hut more comfortable.

There was plenty of Styrofoam available, and so the enclosure and insulation part of the project was quite easy and went well. The next stage of our project was to procure an air conditioner ... not an easy task. Finally we learned that one of the planned reconnaissance missions, required an overnight stop in the Philippines. We talked with the pilot, who agreed to check the Post Exchange, there for an air conditioner he could bring back to DaNang for us. The four of us bought him a couple bottles of whiskey for his trouble, and gave him cash to purchase an air conditioner if one was available.

The pilot went on his mission and when he returned, he had a mid-sized Whirlpool room air conditioner for us. We excitedly cut a hole in the back wall of our insulated hut, and inserted the air conditioner; we plugged it in and turned it on. The lights dimmed, but the air conditioner did nothing. Our investigation revealed that the wiring to the huts was very small ... adequate to power lights and fans, but not capable of providing power necessary for an air conditioner. Pulling the heavier current through these light wires, reduced the voltage so much that the air conditioner could not even start. We were devastated ... what to do now?

After a while we noticed that heavier power lines to the Colonel's house and command center were close to the roof of our hut ... hmm. We debated with ourselves: should we ask, or should we just try to tap-in and ask forgiveness later if necessary? We decided not to ask. But now we had to procure some heavy wire and connectors. We bought another bottle of whiskey, and set off to visit the Seabees ... the military construction people. Sure enough, we found a person there, who provided us with some heavy wire and connectors in exchange for the whiskey. We returned to our hut with the necessary wire and connectors.

Our tallest person with the longest reach, Jim Y put on rubber boots (for electrical insulation), took the wire and connectors and climbed up on top of the metal roof of our hut. We had fashioned a wooden tool for him to snare the wires and pull them toward our hut ... one at a time. With this method he was able to connect the wire we had obtained to the Colonel's power lines. We then ran this wire to our air conditioner. It turned on and started sending cool air into our hut. We were ecstatic! Remarkably we were never questioned about this whole escapade. We don't know whether it was not noticed, or if the Marine officers consciously decided to let us get away with this. The air conditioner was too small to make a major temperature reduction in our hut, but it did reduce the humidity and this provided much needed comfort for us ... especially during the hot summer of 1969.

CHAPTER 11

SUBSTITUTE TEACHER

The Marines had a program where some volunteers would go to residential DaNang to teach English once a week. Grant, a technical representative from another company, was one of my friends and a participant in this education program. The English teachers (primarily Marines) would ride in the back of a 6 by truck to teach for an hour or so at a house in the evening; then after teaching, back to the Marine compound where we lived. The English teachers were unarmed, but there was a driver and another Marine in the front of the truck with shot guns and side-arms. Grant let me know there was a need for a substitute teacher for a period of about a month, and I decided to fill this spot. I was very surprised that when I entered the classroom, the entire class stood up! There were about 20 or 25 Vietnamese civilians in my class ...

ranging from high school to middle age. The "teaching" mainly consisted of demonstrating correct pronunciation, and simple grammar. The students were respectful, eager to learn, and appreciative.

The School

CHAPTER 12

HOA KHANH CHILDREN'S HOSPITAL

One of the students in Grant's class was a very nice young lady named Ana. Ana was working as a nurse at Hoa Khanh Children's Hospital, which was about seven miles away. Ana like many Vietnamese would travel by moped to work and to class. One day Grant told me he was going to Hoa Khanh Hospital, and asked if I would like to come along to see it. Grant had a small motorcycle, and I rode on the back through busy swarms of bikes and mopeds on the road to the hospital.

The hospital was constructed of plywood, screen, and a tin roof, scrounged by Marines. The construction was almost identical to the simple screened-in huts we lived in. The sign at the hospital's entrance was "Love - Happiness - Freedom," It had chalked up an impressive record of accomplishment since February 1967, treating many children as either in or outpatients every month, for a variety of illnesses ranging from worms, cuts and malnutrition to cancer, and plague. The hospital was staffed by Vietnamese nurses and nurse's aides, with help from Marine corpsmen and doctors. The Vietnamese did not listen to the Viet Cong threats and propaganda labeling American doctors as "killers of innocent children," The hospital was very basic though, with many small children crowded together on rough wooden shelves ... more like a warehouse than a western hospital.

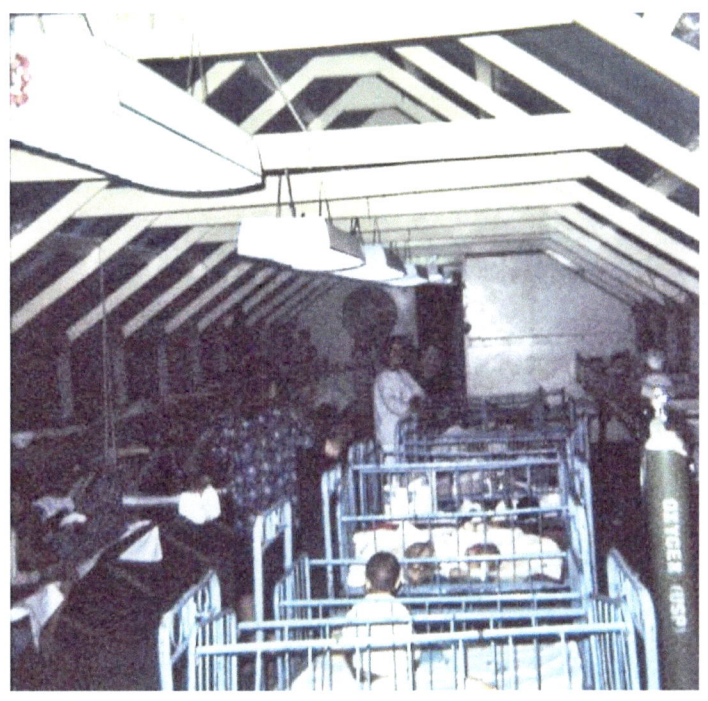

Grant's tour came to an end in two months, and he returned to the US. Before he left, he asked Ana to marry him and come to the US with him. She declined because she could not bear the thought of leaving her family behind.

CHAPTER 13

DaNANG BOMB DUMP EXPLODES

In DaNang, it was a humid, cloudy day about 10:00 in the morning of April, 26 and I was on the flight-line inside the windowless vans of our Elint computer system, when we were rocked by the first huge explosion. I went outside to look around and try to determine what had happened. One huge explosion followed another ... they seemed to be coming from an area several miles away, beyond our living area and beyond Dog Patch, the refugee village adjacent to our living area. With each one, first I would see a large flash that lit up the sky, then I would hear the loud explosion, and finally I would actually see the shock wave moving through the air and a large cloud of smoke at the site of the explosion. This was a frightening illustration of the power of these explosions.

I looked over at the aircraft hangers, and saw that when the shock waves hit the hangers, smooth waves would travel down the huge metal beams above the open aircraft doors. These hangers were very similar to the hangers of today at commercial airports, like MSP. The hangers at DaNang were somewhat smaller, but really good sized, with metal siding, and very heavy steel frames. The steel beams over the aircraft doors must have been at least 24 inch I-beams, necessary to support the wide spans. At the ends of these I-beams, where they attached to vertical steel going to footings in the ground, the beams were held in place; but over the spans above the open doors, smooth waves were clearly visible in these 24 inch beams due to the awesome force of the shock waves. Of course I could feel the force hit my body as well, and after awhile the smell of explosives was in the air. The explosions kept coming; the situation was alarming and frightening, without any announcement of what this was, what to do, or where to go.

This really was quite a display of physics: first the flash ... because light travels so much faster, then the much slower traveling sound, and finally the shock waves traveling slower, but clearly visible going through the air, and finally smooth waves (repetitive oscillations or sine waves) in the large I-beams of the hanger. That "stuff" I learned in physics class was on display.

But what was going on? What was causing this? Were we under attack? We really didn't know. The explosions continued, and sometimes we could see one explosion throw off something which then exploded in mid-air ... a secondary explosion.

After awhile one of the Marine officers speculated that this seemed to be coming from the main bomb dump ... which was indeed beyond our living area and several miles away. The bomb dump was the main storage area for bombs. The bombs were kept there in small piles, separated from other bomb piles by mounds of earth ... theoretically to prevent adjacent piles from exploding if something caused one pile of bombs to explode. The flight line was supplied with bombs ... a few at a time on special carts pulled by a small tractor. Once the bombs were brought to the flight line they were attached to planes, which were then ready to fly combat missions. Well OK that made sense, perhaps the bomb dump was exploding. But why? Had the enemy infiltrated the bomb dump? And was this the beginning of a major attack? We really had no idea.

After watching this for a while, I boarded the truck going back to the living area (about a mile away) to try to find out what was happening. Everyone there had to don their flak jackets and steel helmets, as our living area was closer to the explosions. Yes, the bomb dump was exploding, no one knew why, but now I was feeling some relief that other signs of an attack did not seem to be happening.

It was lunch time, but parts of the roof of the mess hall and kitchen had caved-in due to the explosions. So the cooks were outside with their stoves and grills, making lunch. We had sort of a picnic ... standing around outside, sweating in our flak jackets and helmets, while trying to eat. After lunch I went to our hut and found that the entire back wall had been knocked down and was laying on the ground ... we would fix it later. Inside, everything was in disarray. Anything that had been on a shelf or a table was scattered on the floor.

The "cooking-off" from the bomb dump continued, but at a somewhat slower rate as time passed. It did give me some idea what the enemy experienced when we dropped 500 pound bombs on them! I recall that the last big explosion occurred at midnight, about 14 hours after it had started. Later, it was rumored that a grass fire got away and set off the bomb dump. A very large amount of money went up in smoke that day ... $120 million rumored. I also never did hear how many were injured or killed by these explosions. There was not much said about this whole dramatic incident.

Soon after the bomb dump explosion, there was another spectacular incident when an incoming enemy rocket hit a jet fuel tank located near the flight line. The tank was about the size of the largest grain elevator you have ever seen. The fire lit up the night, and burned for days ... something to behold.

CHAPTER 14

WHEN PIGS FLY

In 1969 one of my "hut mates" in Vietnam was another civilian named Jim Y. He worked for a company that supplied equipment on the F4 Phantom warplanes used by the U.S. military. He split his time: working with MAG11 in DaNang and also working with the Marines of MAG12 at Chu Lai, which was about 60 miles south of DaNang. Jim was an adventurist person. He had previously been in the military, and had been on missions in North Vietnam, where he suffered shrapnel wounds from mortar fire. He had gotten out of the military, but still had some of the shrapnel in his back. He was not easily deterred!

For some reason, in early June Jim had promised to have a Fourth of July pig roast in Chu Lai, for the Marines he worked with there. Unfortunately Jim then learned that there really were no pigs available near Chu Lai or DaNang. Then one evening, Jim was sitting at the bar in the officer's club lamenting his pig roast situation. Next to him at the bar was a CIA Air America pilot, who told Jim that he had seen pigs at a village where he sometimes landed in Laos. Air America flew vintage C47 cargo planes for various missions during the war ... basically versions of the obsolete two engine DC3 passenger planes. Jim asked if he could ride along next time the pilot was going to that village in Laos, and the inebriated pilot agreed.

About a week later, Jim left early in the morning to catch his ride to Laos, in search of pigs for his pig roast. We didn't see Jim again for four days, and we were beginning to think he had been captured or even killed. But late on the fourth day he showed up at the hut ... and was he as mess! He looked haggard; his clothes were filthy, and he smelled like a really bad pig yard.

In due time, Jim told us the story. Sure enough, the pilot did fly him to the village in Laos, but the pilot had to continue-on his route to deliver ammunition and weapons to several other villages. This pilot would not be coming back through the village that day, but he told Jim there would be other Air America planes passing through, and Jim could probably get a ride back on a different plane. So he dropped Jim off and Jim went into the village to look for pigs to buy. He did find a farmer with pigs and purchased two ... on rope leashes. With his two pigs, he then went back out to the airstrip to wait for another

Good Afternoon Vietnam

Air America plane to take him home. Time passed, but no airplane. So Jim basically camped out by the airstrip with his two pigs. The next day a different Air America plane did come through. Jim asked for a ride back to DaNang with his pigs. The pilot said "You've got to be crazy to think you could bring two pigs onto a plane ... they could get loose and really cause a problem ... no way ... forget it," The plane took off, leaving an anxious Jim and his pigs by the side of the airstrip.

"Determined Jim" then went into the village and was able to purchase two metal garbage cans ... one for each pig. Surely he could get on a plane now with the pigs in garbage cans. The next day another CIA plane landed, but again the pilot would not allow Jim to board the plane with his pigs. "They might escape and be loose in the plane," By this time, Jim was getting desperate.

He went into the village and found a USAID medical station. Jim somehow persuaded a nurse to give the pigs shots to immobilize them next time a flight landed. Finally Jim was able to board an Air America flight with the pigs that had been put to sleep in their garbage cans; however his problems were not over. The plane landed in DaNang, but there were Vietnamese officials who would not allow the pigs to be brought into the country. Jim had to persuade the pilot to taxi back out onto the runway and make a special trip to Chu Lai, where there were no such officials. Jim dropped-off his pigs in Chu Lai. He then flew back to DaNang, and came back to our hut after four long days ... thankfully without the pigs!

CHAPTER 15

SOUTHEAST ASIA PHOTO JOURNAL

I have already mentioned that it was necessary to leave the war zone to communicate by phone with my company regarding technical or business issues. These trips to communicate did allow me to sample Southeast Asia, but were quite random depending on when the need to communicate occurred, and where I could "hitch" a ride to. Then there was also the problem of finding a ride back to DaNang. So there were usually a few days wait to return to DaNang. I tried to use this time to learn about the country where I was and also see some interesting things there. On one of my first trips I did buy a book about Southeast Asia, but preparation ahead of time was difficult because I never knew when I would have to go or where I was going ... and usually had very short notice.

I recall that in 1958, Mr. Webb, Social Studies teacher in Faulkton high school had mentioned "things are heating up in Vietnam, Laos, and Cambodia," He said we might be hearing about this in the future ... little did I know. But I do think it was significant that this was part of my education in a little high school in a small village in South Dakota. Other than that I knew very little about Southeast Asia, but I was about to learn more.

Three places I found especially interesting were: Thailand, Singapore, and Taiwan.

This photo of the Golden Image of Buddha, is from Wat Traimitr in Bangkok, Thailand. It weighs five and a half tons of 18 carat gold. Its height is 10 feet; and its width knee to knee is approximately 10 feet. It was created between 1277-1317. For centuries until 1955, it was covered in plaster to hide it from invaders. In 1955 a crane was used to move it, and the plaster cracked, revealing the gold underneath. All of the plaster was then removed, and now it is shown in its original state ... 18 carat gold.

In Bangkok, Thailand there were many old, beautiful, and well preserved Buddhist temples. Also there were Buddhist Monks in their orange robes, with their bowls waiting for people to give them food.

Gary L. Wilhelm

Gary L. Wilhelm

The next photo is of a po tree ... the type of tree Buddha was under in India, when he became enlightened.

And finally in Bangkok, there are many canals. These canals are used for travel and commerce. For example, one could buy a banana from a floating grocery boat that might be going by. There were even gas stations on the canal, so we could stop to fill our outboard motor on our water taxi.

Singapore is another interesting place to visit. The tall white monument is really four columns in Singapore. The four columns memorialize civilians of the four races (Chinese, indigenous Malays, ethnic Indians, and Eurasians) killed there by the Japanese during WWII.

I happened to be in Singapore when they were celebrating their rediscovery by Sir Stamford Raffles 150 years ago. Down by the harbor there were displays of the history and culture, located in large grass huts. The signs explained the celebration.

Grass huts housed the very interesting displays depicting the region over the past 150 years.

To honor the 150 year celebration, Singapore minted $50 commemorative gold coins. I seriously considered getting one, but was worried about bringing it back to the USA when I returned. I knew that at that time our country did not allow bringing gold into the country.

On the streets of Singapore, one could see Indian snake charmers with their baskets of cobras. I didn't go in for a close look, but this was interesting ... only from a distance, for me.

Tiger Balm is an Asian product that is similar to Vicks Vapor Rub. The Tiger Balm Company created a Tiger Balm Garden in Singapore, which depicts Chinese Legends using figures made of painted concrete. Mythical figures from the legends decorate the garden. My understanding is there is a Tiger Balm Garden in Hong Kong as well.

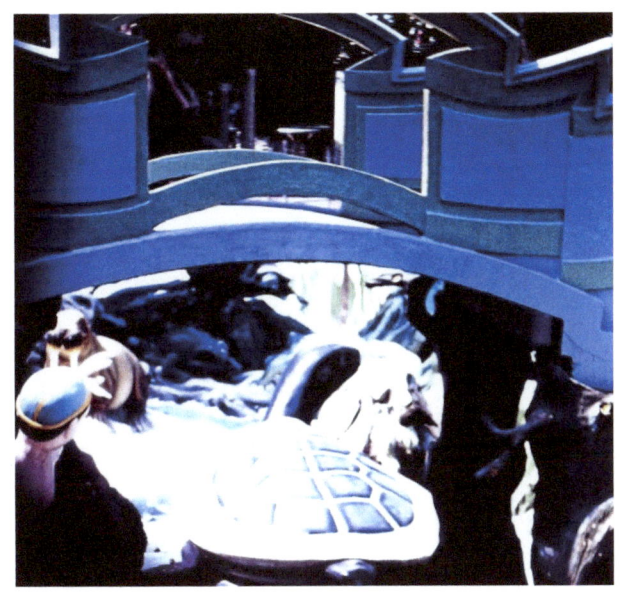

The Singapore Botanical Gardens were another spot I visited. Many beautiful jungle orchids were there.

Also, sealing wax palm trees were a surprise to me. These palm trees provided the wax used to seal important documents for many years.

While in Singapore, I did take a brief field trip across the border to the Muslim country of Malaysia. The mosque was quite beautiful with elaborate prayer rugs.

Another thing of interest was a Malaysian grade school in a small village. It was very small with corrugated metal for a roof, and the sides were primarily screen. Instead of a teacher there was a television set ... the lessons were delivered via television! I don't believe there was a village teacher, just a monitor. I was able to visit a mosque and a village school.

And finally for Singapore there is the Raffles Hotel, named after Sir Stamford Raffles. A number of famous authors had stayed (even lived at) the Raffles. These included Joseph Conrad, Somerset Maughm, and Michner. Some of them wrote "south seas" books while they were there. One afternoon I went to the Raffles. I didn't write anything there, but to honor the occasion, I had a

Singapore Sling ... a drink I had never tried before. It wasn't bad.

Now on to Taipei, Taiwan. When Chaing and his nationalists fled Mao and the communist troops in China for safety on Taiwan, they took many art objects, and valuables with them. Most of these are preserved and hidden in caves, but a few at a time are brought out and displayed in the National Museum shown below. The displays I saw were many pieces of beautifully carved Jade. However one thing I noticed were some rather peculiar bowls. I asked about these and was told they were made from the skulls of Hinata Buddhist monks that had died. It turns out that these Buddhists check the skulls of their monks who die to see how smooth they are. They believe that if the monks have been pious and spent enough time meditating, the surface of their skulls will be very smooth. If the smoothness criteria is passed, then the skulls are made into these bowls to be used in religious services.

Next is the National Museum to dinner theater, which is spectacular in Taipei. The food was good, and there was a big variety of amazing entertainment. Of course the Chinese are famous for acrobatics, but there was also music, and groups dancing in costume. The entertainment included a wide range of acts.

Gary L. Wilhelm

Now, just to mention several opportunities I had, but missed out on: Hong Kong, Angkor Wat, and Hue.

Although Hong Kong was somewhat hard for me to get to, I learned that a Navy group with a base down the field from us, occasionally flew to Hong Kong. They gathered intelligence somewhat like our VMCJ squadron. Our intelligence gathering was done with a two person plane and was tactical ... focusing only on missions within Vietnam. The Navy operation was strategic and used much larger EC121 planes with 30 or more people on board, including language specialists who would translate conversations they overheard. This Navy unit flew out of and between two bases, DaNang and Atsugi, Japan. At one point, I learned they had a flight planned with a stop in Hong Kong, and requested to ride along. They said "sure," However they had to change their schedule, and I did not get word of the change.

On April 15, 1969 North Korean Mig fighter planes came out 90 miles, over international waters, and shot down one of the Navy intelligence gathering planes. Thirty Navy personnel and one Marine were on board, and all perished. This was not the flight I had planned to take to Hong Kong, but after hearing about this, I gave up the idea of going to Hong Kong on one of these Navy flights.

When I was in Bangkok, I learned of tours to Angkor Wat in Cambodia. I had to choose whether to spend my time in Bangkok, or try to work in a tour of Angkor Wat. I also learned the

Cambodian tours sometimes encountered armed bandits on the way to Angkor Wat, so Bangkok was probably the best decision.

Finally during the 1968 Tet Offensive, the North Vietnamese had captured Hue, and slaughtered thousands of people. Before I arrived at DaNang, Hue had been recaptured and was held by Marines. My friend, Grant, had made arrangements with Marines to go along on a helicopter mission so he could see Hue, and I could have gone also. This was undoubtedly another once-in-a-lifetime opportunity that I chose not to take.

My need to go outside the war zone to communicate did allow me to sample some interesting places in Southeast Asia. Overall, I found this part of the world fascinating.

CHAPTER 16

MARINE CORPS BIRTHDAY PARTY 1969

I was invited to attend the Marine Corps Birthday Party at the officer's club in DaNang. I had been invited to the party in North Carolina before we left for DaNang, but did not attend because I lacked a tuxedo and did not know where to rent one there. But this time in DaNang, I dug out the blue suit I had worn on my trip over, and attended. That was the best I could do.

There were many toasts, and interesting historical references. It was well worthwhile. I had developed a lot of respect for the Marines, and felt relatively safe with them, even in a war zone. They are very good at what they do, are patriotic, disciplined, brave, and live up to their tradition.

CHAPTER 17

SURPRISE OFFER FROM THE CLEANING LAUNDRY LADY

Just a few days before I left Vietnam, our cleaning lady said she wanted to talk with me. She showed me two pictures ... one of a very young beautiful girl, and the other of a can of Budweiser beer. She handed me the picture of the girl first and said: "This is my daughter, for you ... she is cherry (a virgin)," Then she gave me the photo of the can of Budweiser, and said: "you come to my house," I was very surprised, and somewhat taken aback. I knew she had come from the North because she was Catholic and had been persecuted there. I didn't even know she had a daughter, or where she lived, but I presumed she lived in Dogpatch. I knew I would be leaving very soon. I pondered for a few minutes ... what do I do?

What should I say? I told her I was very sorry but I could not leave the compound at this point. She seemed to have sensed that I would be leaving Vietnam soon. She asked if she could have my umbrella and a couple of other things. I gave them to her. She said she believed my other hut mates would fire her after I was gone. I told her "Oh no," but they probably did. They were much less tolerant of her crabbiness, but if I had to live in Dogpatch, I would be crabby too.

CHAPTER 18

GOING HOME

I had been the sole Univac engineer there for months now. My first associate from Univac had been medevac'd with a seriously broken arm. His replacement had been sent over after a delay of several weeks. He had committed to stay for six months and that is exactly what he did. After six months he left, and I had been the lone Univac representative since then. Univac apparently could not come up with his replacement. However I had been there much longer than even the Marines were required to stay, so I had been writing and requesting to leave. Univac would respond to everything else, but they acted like my requests to come home somehow did not get through ... no mention, no answer. I wanted to be home for Christmas. Every day I waited at the post office for the letter that would give me a departure date. The Marines saw this and realized what Univac was doing. Finally, the commanding office wrote me orders to go ahead and go home in late November. I was very grateful.

Gary L. Wilhelm

I took my orders with my few possessions and got on a military plane for Tokyo, via the Philippines. When I arrived in Tokyo, I called the company. Their telephone response was "Oh Gary, calm down ... take a couple weeks off ... tour Japan, call us back after that and we'll talk about it," I got off the phone, and immediately made plans to take a flight to San Francisco the next day. Once in SF, I called and said "I'm in San Francisco. Do you believe me now?"

CHAPTER 19

CONCLUSIONS

When I returned to the USA, my primary reaction was joy at being back, and in one piece. However my job for the past two years had taken me out of the mainstream. Once back at work, I was able to transfer to a different department at Univac and have a continuing job, and for that I was grateful. In spite of all the positive aspects of being back I did have some difficulty adjusting, and I'm not sure why. Maybe it was that I hadn't driven for many months, and now I had to drive through traffic to work. Then I would sit behind a desk all day. Within a few months I realized that to get the kind of position I wanted, I would need to do something different. I ended up going back to graduate school to get a master's degree in electrical engineering, and that helped me get back in the game.

Another thing I pondered was: "Was it worthwhile to me?" There was extra compensation, and a reduced cost of living. The compensation was definitely not even close to what the mercenaries of today (like Blackwater) are paid, but the danger was less too. I did have an opportunity to visit a number of countries in the Orient, and see a diversity of cultures and religions. I think this was beneficial. I also saw people without access to clean water or plumbing, who lived and worked without obvious complaining. I did come back relatively intact, so it could have been much worse. Two years of my life for this ... would I do it again ... probably no. War is terrible and a wise person would stay as far away from it as possible!

The other part of this worthwhile question is: "How was our ELINT system worthwhile for our military personnel and our national defense?" Although our technology was new, it provided another tool along with older technology, experience and first-hand knowledge for the Marines. All new technology requires some time for full acceptance. I believe our 1968 technology was probably an important step to newer systems we have developed since then. Perhaps the two most important contributions in 1968/1969 were: providing rapid information on movement of enemy weapons, and detecting new more powerful equipment provided to North Vietnam by the Russians. Information about new Russian weapons systems was immediately sent to the Defense Intelligence Agency, DIA.

For a long time, I had been hearing from the generals through the media about body counts, and their certainty that we were winning. The problem is: that was our general's criteria for winning, not the criteria of North Vietnam. The general's and politician's failure to realize we were not winning, along with misconceptions like the "domino theory" cost many lives and much treasure. The war was certainly asymmetrical. The enemy delivered many of their low-cost weapons by bicycle on trails from the north. Many of our weapons cost tens of millions of dollars each. I am writing this after the end of the war, but when I returned it was not yet finished. Now I know the war certainly did not end well ... not only for the US but also for many really good Vietnamese people, who had worked with us, fought with us, and were let down in the end.

Right away when I came back, I did develop a more keen interest in the news, and a realization that different channels put different slants on the news. I have since decided to listen to several channels and take an average (with my personal weighting), especially about important issues. Today this is even more necessary than when I returned in 1969.

I had been naively under the impression that if I were badly hurt or even disabled, the company and company insurance would take care of me, similar to the military. But I was skeptical enough to have my pay stubs sent to a relative for safekeeping while I was gone. When I returned I added these up and discovered that my pay was about $1300 short. I asked the company about this, and they assured me that they had paid me correctly. Only after taking the pay stubs in and going through all of them, did they pay the $1300 they owed me. Well this, along with the failure of the company to answer me when I asked to come home, destroyed my confidence in the company and company insurance. The Veterans Administration covers military personnel; civilians are not covered by the VA. This is another reason for civilians to stay away from wars.

I guess being taught to be less naive is a valuable fringe benefit too. Maybe it was all worthwhile in a strange way.

Good Afternoon Vietnam

CEASE-FIRE!
All GIs Out of Viet in 60 Days

STARS AND STRIPES

AN AUTHORIZED UNOFFICIAL PUBLICATION
FOR THE U.S. ARMED FORCES OF THE PACIFIC COMMAND   10¢

Vol. 29, No. 24   Thursday, Jan. 25, 1973

WASHINGTON — President Nixon announced Tuesday night that a Vietnam cease-fire will go into effect Saturday night with all American troops to be withdrawn within 60 days, coinciding with return of all American prisoners.

The announcement was made simultaneously in Washington, Saigon and Hanoi.

Nixon said agreement has been reached with North Vietnam to end the Indochina War "with honor."

Nixon said the agreement was initialed in Paris earlier Tuesday by Henry A. Kissinger, his chief Vietnam negotiator, and Hanoi's Le Duc Tho. He said it would go into effect at 7 p.m. EST Saturday.

Nixon said the agreement would "end the war and bring peace with honor in Southeast Asia."

In a nationwide address to the nation Nixon read a statement which he said was being simultaneously issued by North

Related story, Page 3

Family, Friends Gather in Austin To Honor LBJ

AUSTIN, Tex. — The people who knew former

Vietnamese officials which ex-

ABOUT THE AUTHOR

Gary L. Wilhelm is a retired engineer with a master's degree from South Dakota State University, who did research and development work in America, Asia, and Europe for consumer, commercial, and military products, during a career of several decades. In addition to being a civilian engineer embedded with the Marines during the Vietnam War in 1968 and 1969, he worked developing products ranging from EF Johnson citizens band radio, and the Texas Instruments home computer, communications technology for use within buildings, and with medical devices implanted within the body, to the Howitzer Improvement Program (HIP) for army artillery on the battlefield. He was also a representative on a North Atlantic Treaty Organization (NATO) committee, and hosted the USA meeting of the committee at Honeywell.

https://www.mnvietnam.org/story/good-afternoon-vietnam-my-first-afternoon-there/ http://www.reminiscing-writers.com/
https://twitter.com/GaryLWilhelm
https://gary-l-wilhelm-author.com/

REVIEWS

Review on Amazon UK by Crystal McClean

I'm going to start off by saying that I am NOT a fan of war stories...BUT this book is DIFFERENT! Good Afternoon Vietnam is not a story about war, nor is it a story of a soldier. This is a story about a young man in a blue suit, white shirt, and tie who has left academia and is beginning his venture into the real world as an engineer; and little did he know how real that world would become. An initial request to transfer to Iceland (which was turned down) led him to two years in the heart of Vietnam.

Wilhelm's descriptions tell the tale well...the heat, the humidity, the smell, as he departed the plane into a land unknown. Being surrounded by armed military men while he was neither military nor armed. He uses the vernacular where appropriate, but explains what the terminology means.

This is a story not particularly violent (except for an unseen bar fight), but rather of adventure; making the best of what you have to improve life, of dull days at work, and watching love bloom between others.

Wilhelm was overwhelmed at the war life when he arrived in Vietnam and didn't take a photo for months as he didn't want to remember what he was seeing. However, I'm glad that he finally did take some photos, as they are sprinkled throughout this book so that we can catch a small glimpse of tin shacks covered in Styrofoam and just picture in our minds some of the hi-jinx he and his friends managed...after all, Wilhelm was an engineer so what else would he do in his down time other than find ways to install unapproved air conditioning?

Ways of communicating with friends and bosses were less than ideal in times before encrypted sat phones and the internet. Just imagine having to fly out of the country to make a phone call! Alcohol was used as currency, and even going to buy toothpaste could involve danger. Yes, this was a whole other world in another time, and one that I know little about, but am now more curious to learn more of.

These are stories that have long been told to Wilhelm's family and friends, no doubt, but are now written down and preserved and shared so that we can see a side of conflict rarely publicly known. It's an easy read and I can imagine being around a table with him while he's retelling a little bit here and there as asides into general conversation.

Good Afternoon Vietnam has been a delight to read and I look forward to seeing more from this author in the future. I know that this man in a blue suit, white shirt, and tie certainly has many more interesting tales to tell of life in the real world.

Review by Dr. Theodore J. Cohen

Gary Wilhelm hits it out of the park with his first-hand account of his work in RVN during the war.

Even though he was a civilian, parts of this story sound like they came directly from the television series M*A*S*H (which, of course, hearkens back to the Korean Police Action of the early 1950s). Wilhelm's trials and tribulations in performing his job (having to leave the country just to communicate with his company in the States? What was that about???!), much less the effort it took to perform the things we take for granted as we go about our daily lives (e.g., shopping), would have been enough to drive most people mad.

My hat's off to you, Gary; thank you for your service! What a great read. Anyone interested in what really went on behind the scenes during the war in RVN will not want to miss this book. It's a fast--and very enjoyable--read!

Five stars, all the way.

Public Domain Photos

https://pxhere.com/en/photo/1017455

https://en.wikipedia.org/wiki/Flag_of_the_United_States_Marine_Corps

https://en.wikipedia.org/wiki/Flag_of_South_Vietnam

https://www.flickr.com/photos/13476480@N07/15893495474

www.ingramcontent.com/pod-product-compliance
Lightning Source LLC
Chambersburg PA
CBHW042322150426
43192CB00001B/23